"Now Jacob loved Joseph more than all his children…
and he made him a coat of many colors…

And when his brethren saw that their father loved him
more than all his brethren, they hated him, and could not
speak peaceably unto him…" Genesis 37: 3-4

First published in Great Britain in 2004 by Frances Lincoln Children's Books,
4 Torriano Mews, Torriano Avenue, London NW5 2RZ
www.franceslincoln.com

This edition published in 2004 under license from Frances Lincoln Limited
by Eerdmans Books for Young Readers,
an imprint of Wm. B. Eerdmans Publishing Co.,
255 Jefferson SE, Grand Rapids, Michigan 49503
P.O. Box 163, Cambridge CB39PU U.K.

A catalog record of this book is available from the Library of Congress.

ISBN 0-8028-5277-7

Set in Minion

Printed in Singapore
05 06 07 08 09 10   9 8 7 6 5 4 3 2

THE COAT
OF MANY COLORS

Jenny Koralek
Illustrated by Pauline Baynes

EERDMANS BOOKS FOR YOUNG READERS
GRAND RAPIDS, MICHIGAN   CAMBRIDGE, U.K.

The coat of many colors was very special. Finely, finely spun, it was woven out of the softest wool from the best sheep. Light as air, it was embroidered with desert flowers in fiery silks and strewn with crescent moons, midday suns, and evening stars in threads of silver and gold. Anyone who saw it longed to wear it.

One day long ago, a man called Jacob gave the coat to his son Joseph. Jacob had many other sons, but he loved Joseph best.

Little did he know how much trouble this coat would cause.

Joseph's ten half-brothers were jealous of him because he was Jacob's favorite. They were also angry because he never helped them in the fields. But above all, they hated Joseph because of his dreams.

Once he told them, "I dreamed that you were sheaves of corn bowing down to one great sheaf of corn – which was me!" Another time he said, "I dreamed that the sun, moon, and all the stars were bowing down to me. The sun was our father, the moon was my mother, and you were the stars. My dreams say that one day I will be a very important person."

The brothers grew tired of hearing about Joseph's dreams. So one day, when they saw him prancing towards them in his coat of many colors, they decided to get rid of him.

"Let's kill the dreamer!" they said.

"No! No!" cried the eldest brother, Reuben. "Don't kill him! Let's throw him into that empty well and leave him there for a while. That will teach him a lesson."

So the brothers tore the coat of many colors off Joseph's back, gave him a beating, and flung him down the well.

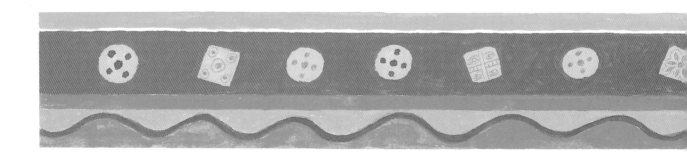

"You can cool off there," they shouted, "and learn to mend your ways!"

Reuben could not bear to hear Joseph's cries coming from the well.

He went away and hid, waiting for a chance to rescue his brother.

Joseph lay in the dark well – hungry, cold, thirsty,
battered, and bruised.

"If ever I get out of here," he vowed, "I will never,
never boast about anything again."

Then a long line of camels appeared through the desert haze.

"Look!" cried one of the brothers. "Here come some merchants carrying spices down to Egypt. Let's sell our pretty Joseph as a slave!"

"Good idea!" said the others. So they sold Joseph to the merchants for twenty pieces of silver.

When Reuben came back, he was horrified. "What have you done?" he shouted. "Do you want to break our father's heart?"

Then the brothers realized what a terrible thing they had done.

"Oh, Reuben," they wailed, "what shall we tell our father?"

"We shall have to lie to him," said Reuben sadly.

The brothers smeared the tattered coat of many colors with goat's blood and told Jacob that Joseph had been killed by a wild beast. And their father believed them. Day and night he wept for Joseph and would not be comforted.

Joseph was now a slave in Egypt. But not for long.

The Pharaoh was having worrying dreams of seven fat cows and seven thin cows, seven plump ears of corn and seven empty ears of corn. His wise men could not tell him what they meant. Then one day his cup-bearer said, "O Great One, not long ago I had a dream. A slave told me what it meant – and it came true exactly as he said it would."

"Send for this man at once!" commanded the Pharaoh.

Joseph came and knelt before the Pharaoh.

"O Great One," he said, "your dreams are telling you
to store all the corn in Egypt while the harvest is good,
because there is going to be a terrible famine."

The Pharaoh listened to Joseph's advice. He even put him
in charge of the corn stores. When the bad harvests came,
no one in Egypt starved and the grateful Pharaoh heaped
rich rewards on Joseph.

But famine did come to the land where Jacob lived, and he sent his sons to Egypt to buy corn.

The brothers did not recognize Joseph in his robes of purple and gold, but Joseph recognized them. And while they were filling their sacks with corn, he hid a precious silver cup in his little brother Benjamin's sack.

When Joseph's soldiers searched the sacks at the Egyptian border,
they found the silver cup. They arrested the brothers and took them
straight back to Joseph.

"Benjamin must stay here," ordered Joseph, "but the rest of you may go."

"This is a punishment for what we did to Joseph," the brothers said
to one another, not knowing that Joseph understood what they were saying.

They fell to their knees.

"Keep us here, but please let Benjamin go home," they begged. "You see, our brother Joseph died long ago and it broke our father's heart. If he never sees Benjamin again, it will surely kill him."

Then Joseph knew that his brothers had changed as much as he had.

"Don't you recognize me?" he said. "I am Joseph!"

His astonished brothers bowed low before him.

"Forgive us, Joseph, for what we did to you," they said.

Joseph hugged his brothers.

"Of course I forgive you," he said. "We have all learned many lessons since I first put on the coat of many colors. And now, go and bring our dear father to me. Then we can all share my good fortune in this land of plenty."

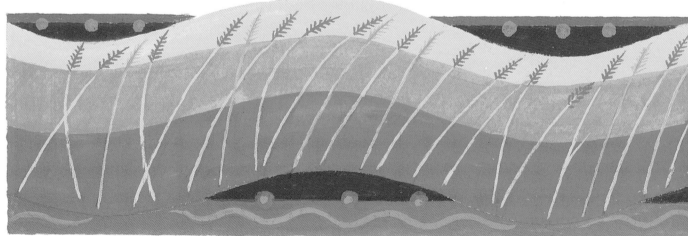